MW00951030

CREATIVE CONTRIBUTORS

REVERSE
COLORING BOOK
FOR KIDS

Welcome to our Reverse Coloring Book.

This book has 50 watercolor designs
without ANY outlines or details!

These pages are designed to allow your imagination to run
wild and it's totally up to you what you do on each page.

Remember, there is no right or wrong way!

Have fun!!

How It Works

With each image comes a new opportunity to express your inner artist. All you need is a pen, we recommend a thin black pen to begin with, but feel free to use whatever instruments you like!

Because remember, there are no rules!

But to get you started, below are some ideas to what you can do...

Outline	Double Outline	Shading	Doodles

Inner Lines	Partial Shading	Faces	Squiggles

Lines	Blocks	Dots	Writing

An Example

Below is a quick example of how you can approach each image by drawing, tracing, doodling and letting your creativity run away.

CREATIVE CONTRIBUTORS

REVERSE
COLORING BOOK
FOR KIDS

Thank You!

We hope you enjoyed the book!

If you enjoyed it you can find more of our books at:
bit.ly/creativecontributors

or by scanning the QR code below!

Made in the USA
Las Vegas, NV
29 December 2024

15568975R00059